THE
★ R
COOKBOOK

ALEX BARKER

Published in association with
the US Rice Council

A MARTIN BOOK

Published by Martin Books
an imprint of Woodhead-Faulkner Ltd
Fitzwilliam House, 32 Trumpington Street
Cambridge CB2 1QY
in association with the US Rice Council

First published 1986
© Woodhead-Faulkner Ltd 1986
ISBN 0 85941 365 9

British Library Cataloguing in Publication Data

Barker, Alex
  The American rice cookbook.
  1. Cookery (Rice)
  I. Title II. US Rice Council
  641.6'318   TX809.R5

  ISBN 0-85941-365-9

Design: Carrods Graphic Design, Cambridge
Photography: Melvin Grey
Food preparation for photography: Lesley Scott
Cover preparation: Anne Dettmer
Typesetting: Jill Wood Typesetting, Cambridge
Printed and bound in Great Britain by Springbourne Press
Limited, Basildon, Essex

Foreword

For many years in Britain, rice was used mainly to make rice puddings or as an accompaniment to a curry. However, British cooking has undergone many changes which have resulted in the emergence of an increased and adventurous use of rice. This, we feel, is largely because British holidaymakers are travelling abroad more and now have the opportunity to sample the cuisine of other countries.

The majority of foreign cuisines have one thing in common—the interesting and delicious ways in which they utilise rice. In addition, the many foreign restaurants situated in our own high streets have made it possible for diners to establish their enjoyment of these exciting new tastes. British cooks recognise the potential of rice, too. Now more adventurous in the kitchen, they are willing to try new ideas when cooking with it. And the quality and reliability of American rice cannot be overlooked.

It is for these reasons that the US Rice Council asked Alex Barker, known to you for many years as Cookery Editor of *Woman's Own*, to write a cookbook and devise recipes using American rice. We have been rewarded with a book rich in variety, novelty and plain good sense that shows clearly how American rice fits into everyday use, whether it be for family meals or fancy entertaining.

We hope you enjoy this book and feel certain that many of the recipes in it will become firm favourites with both your family and your friends.

Anne Dettmer
RICE INFORMATION SERVICE
on behalf of the US Rice Council

Introduction

I t all stems from a simple grain. A grain which, on cooking, trebles in volume and will absorb many flavours and colours. A grain which has an enormous variety of uses and contains many vital, everyday nutrients. This simple grain is rice—the staff of life for East and West alike—and yet little is known about rice grown in America.

Rice has been cultivated in the United States for around 300 years and is recognised throughout the world as the best. It is grown in the five Southern States of Arkansas, Louisiana, Mississippi, Missouri and Texas and in the Western State of California.

It is not by pure coincidence that rice has become a staple food throughout the world; in fact, it is real common sense. This economical and versatile food fits in well with today's views on healthy eating: rice is low in calories—just 35 calories per cooked ounce, 105 calories per raw ounce—it's low in fat, free of cholesterol and very low in salt. It also contains some B vitamins, calcium, phosphorus and iron, and so provides the basis for a very healthy meal.

From all around the world come different cuisines which have had strong influences on rice cookery. For instance, the hot and peppery creole cooking of the Southern United States; the very hot chilli cooking of Mexico; the infinitely varied spiced cookery of the Middle East; the fresh, crisp and aromatic cookery of the Orient, and the long, slow, moist cooking of Italian risottos. All can be shown at their best with American rice, and many have been used in this book, hopefully to bring interesting cooking and enjoyable eating to everyone.

Raspberry Rice Ring (Page 94);
Iced Rice Cheesecake (Page 95)

Types of American rice

There are many types of American rice available.

1 REGULAR MILLED LONG GRAIN WHITE RICE. The husk, bran and germ of the rice have been removed. The grain is slim and four to five times as long as it is wide.

2 PARBOILED RICE (sometimes called pre-fluffed or easy cook rice). This rice has been subjected to a steam-pressure process which helps the rice to retain much of its natural vitamin and mineral content. This process also hardens the grain, reducing the possibility of overcooking. Raw, it is slightly more yellow than regular white rice, but, when cooked, it has the same white appearance.

3 BROWN RICE (also known as whole grain rice). This is rice with the bran layer intact; only the husk has been removed. Some of the brown rice on sale is quick-cooking, so always check the packet instructions for recommended cooking times. All brown rice referred to in this book is long grain.

4 SHORT GRAIN RICE. This is a regular milled pudding rice which is short and fat in shape and chalky white in colour. It is a softer rice than those previously mentioned and, when cooked, the grains stick together (unlike the grains of the other rices above, which remain separate on cooking).

5 WILD RICE. This is not a true rice at all but an aquatic grass. The grains are long and slim and range from dark brown to black in colour. If you find wild rice difficult to obtain, you may substitute either brown or white rice in any of the recipes given. Check when substituting with the rice chart on page 7 for appropriate cooking time.

6 LONG GRAIN AND WILD RICE MIX. Wild rice is very expensive, but it is possible to buy it mixed with long grain rice to make it go further.

7 CANNED RICE. Long grain and brown (whole grain) rice are available in cans ready-cooked, needing only a further 3 minutes to heat through before serving.

8 FROZEN RICE. A very recent addition to the market, frozen rice is available in brown or white varieties. It also requires about 3 minutes' preparation time.

How to cook American rice

Rice cooking can be as easy as pie so long as you follow a few simple guidelines. First of all, be sure not to overcook the rice. Cook it in a pan with a very tight-fitting lid. Don't wash or rinse American rice either before or after cooking as there is no need. Add only the amount of water stated: too much water will almost always lead to overcooked or soggy rice. Finally, cook it very slowly, otherwise the water will have evaporated before the rice is cooked.

Put the rice, water and salt to taste into a saucepan. Bring to the boil, lower the heat to simmer, and stir once. Cover the pan and cook for the length of time recommended in the table below.

TYPE OF RICE	QUANTITY OF RICE	QUANTITY OF WATER	COOKING TIME
Long grain	1 cup/8 oz/225 g	2 cups/1 pint/500 ml	15 minutes
Parboiled	1 cup/8 oz/225 g	$2\frac{1}{2}$ cups/$1\frac{1}{4}$ pints/625 ml	20–25 minutes
Brown	1 cup/8 oz/225 g	2 cups/1 pint/500 ml	35–45 minutes
Wild	1 cup/8 oz/225 g	2 cups/1 pint/500 ml	45 minutes
Short grain	$\frac{1}{2}$ cup/4 oz/100 g	2 cups/1 pint/500 ml	up to 1 hour

Don't be tempted to check the rice too often while it is cooking as you will let out steam and therefore moisture. Don't rinse the rice when it is cooked; just fluff it up with a fork to serve. A little knob of butter or oil and seasoning may be added if you wish. To keep rice hot after cooking, place it in a collander over a pan of gently simmering water and cover it until you want it.

Short grain rice for puddings is often baked slowly in the oven. You can, however, cook it on top of the cooker, either in a double saucepan or in a heavy-based pan with a lid. Short grain rice needs to be cooked until it is quite soft and it will be after about 30 minutes, but generally, when making a pudding, it is better to cook it for about 1 hour.

IN A PRESSURE COOKER. Follow the quantities given in the table above and bring to the boil in the pressure cooker base. Stir once, fix on the cover and bring to high (15 lb) pressure. Lower the heat and cook white rice for 5 minutes, brown rice for 8 minutes and pudding rice for 12 minutes. Reduce the pressure and continue as usual.

IN A SLOW COOKER. Follow the quantities given in the table above. Place the rice, salt, boiling water and a knob of butter in the slow cooker. Cover and cook on the highest setting for $1-1\frac{1}{2}$ hours. (This gives a softer, less fluffy result than cooking in the ordinary way.)

In a Rice Cooker. Follow the quantities given in the table above. Place the rice, salt and boiling water in the cooker, bring back to the boil and cover. When the liquid has been absorbed by the rice, the cooker will automatically turn itself off.

In a Microwave Oven. Follow the quantities given in the table above. Place the rice, water and salt in a very large microwave-proof container. Cover and cook for 15 minutes on full power. Remove and allow the rice to stand, covered, for another 5 minutes.

Cooked rice freezes well both on its own and in sauces and cooked dishes. Reheat complete dishes as recommended for that recipe. Reheat rice alone, either in the oven, dotted with a little oil or butter and covered, or gently in a pan with a little water.

Flavouring, colouring and shaping American rice

Rarely will you serve rice absolutely *au naturel*, with nothing added at all. Even as the simplest accompaniment, rice is best enhanced with a little seasoning or butter or oil, tossed in as soon as it is just cooked. But as rice takes so well to other liquids, flavours, seasonings, colours and shapes, it makes an even more tasty and interesting accompaniment if you do a little of your own experimenting.

1 Cooking Liquids. Any liquid can be used which will enhance the recipe or main dish the rice is accompanying, be it milk or fruit juices for desserts, or stock, cider, beer, wine or a mixture of these for savoury dishes.

2 Colours. Many recipes call for the use of saffron threads, but these are so expensive. Turmeric powder can be used instead. If you do wish to use saffron, soak 1 teaspoon of saffron threads in 2—3 tablespoons of boiling water for 10 minutes. Stir this liquid into the rice and its cooking liquid at the beginning of the cooking time, and then cook as usual. Other colours can be obtained either by the addition of paprika pepper (which will also give a spicy taste) or brightly coloured fruit juices, for example, or by using a few drops of food colouring. For children's parties, it is often fun to give rice a totally new look and a new colour.

Corn Mountain with Prawns and Pimento Sauce (Page 90); Jambalaya (Page 38)

3 FLAVOURS. Rice absorbs flavours both during cooking and immediately after, so if you cook it quite plainly try some of these quick and tasty serving additions: fried onions and garlic; any chopped fresh herbs; chilli powder; chopped blanched peppers or other crisp vegetables; peeled, chopped tomatoes and a little fresh basil; black pepper and grated cheese and butter; chopped dried fruits or nuts; toasted seeds such as sesame or sunflower.

4 SHAPELY RICE. It is certainly not a new idea to shape rice: it has been done for centuries in many Latin American and Middle Eastern cuisines. Not only can it give a totally different presentation to many rice dishes, but it can also be a good way of portioning food. As an attractive way to serve rice, especially for a buffet table, it requires no extra effort at all. Just pack the cooked and flavoured rice into individual moulds (or ramekin dishes) or into one larger mould and leave it for about 5 minutes. Place the mould on a plate, give it a quick, short tap on the underside, and the rice will slide out. For large quantities, or if you are unsure of unmoulding the rice easily, line the mould with clingfilm the first couple of times you try it.

SYMBOLS USED IN THE BOOK

Ⓕ denotes a recipe suitable for freezing

Ⓥ denotes a vegetarian recipe

Recipe Index

Brandy Rice Alaska (Page 96);
Jewels in a Crown (Pages 94—5)

Family Favourites

This selection of recipes includes some variations of firm family favourites as well as many new ideas. They are all ideal for everyday family meals, both for children and adults, although some may be more suited to family Sunday lunches or the main meal of the week. There are ideas for your vegetarian family or friends, which can also be turned into non-vegetarian dishes or starters and light meals. You will also find many dishes that are geared to saving the pennies and using up left-overs, not only of rice, but of many other everyday foods. And, of course, there are puddings too. You won't find a traditional rice pudding, but there are other delicious ideas to tempt you and the kids and fill many a hungry tummy.

Chicken Polo

Serves 6

Preparation time: about 1 hour

Cooking time: 1 hour

Ⓕ (add extra stock when reheating)

Polo is an Iranian rice dish, not unlike a pilaff, in which all the ingredients are cooked with the rice, either in the oven or on the top of the cooker. It has a crunchy brown rice crust at the bottom, as a result of adding a yogurt and butter mixture before layering.

$2\frac{1}{2}$–3 lb (1.25–1.5 kg) chicken in portions

salt and black pepper

1 large onion, quartered

14 oz (400 g) American long grain rice

1 orange

5 oz (125 g) butter

3 carrots, grated

3 oz (75 g) flaked almonds

2 oz (50 g) sugar

2 teaspoons fresh root ginger, grated, *or* 1 teaspoon ground ginger
$\frac{1}{2}$ teaspoon ground turmeric
3 tablespoons natural yogurt
1 oz (25 g) pistachio nuts, shelled, to serve

Put the chicken in a large pan with the seasoning and onion, and sufficient water to cover. Cover with a tight-fitting lid and cook gently for 15 minutes or until the chicken is tender. Remove the flesh from the bones and keep the stock.

Meanwhile, pour the rice into a pan of salted boiling water and cook, briskly, for 5 minutes. Drain and keep hot.

Cut the rind off the orange and cut it into very thin strips. Place these strips in a small pan of boiling water and boil for 1 minute. Drain.

Melt 4 oz (100 g) butter in a small pan and add the grated carrot. Cook for a couple of minutes and then add the orange rind, almonds, sugar, ginger and turmeric. Stir over a low heat until the sugar has dissolved. Cover tightly and simmer for 5—10 minutes.

Melt the remaining butter, and mix this and 2 tablespoons of water with the yogurt. Pour into the base of a heavy casserole with a tight-fitting lid. Spread half the rice over the base of the casserole, then half the carrot mixture and then the chicken flesh. Cover the chicken with the rest of the rice and top with the remaining carrot mixture. Cover tightly and cook in a pre-heated oven at 180°C (350°F, Gas Mark 4) for about 1 hour. Pour on $\frac{1}{4}$ pint (125 ml) chicken cooking liquid half-way through cooking. Serve sprinkled with the pistachio nuts.

Garlicky Turkey Drumstick

Serves 2–3

Preparation time: 20 minutes

Cooking time: 50 minutes

1 turkey drumstick, boned*

4 oz (100 g) American long grain rice

2 oz (50 g) garlic butter

1 tablespoon chopped parsley

lemon juice

salt and freshly ground black pepper

2–3 tablespoons dry white wine, optional

1 oz (25 g) butter, optional

*Ask your butcher to bone the drumstick for you when you order it, but ask him to keep it in one piece so that you can stuff it with the rice filling.

Cook the rice as directed on page 7, but for only 10 minutes. Drain it and immediately add half the butter, the parsley and a teaspoon of lemon juice and toss well. Add the rest of the butter in chunks and pack this filling into the turkey drumstick, placed on a piece of foil. Sprinkle with seasoning and squeeze on a little more lemon juice. Wrap tightly in the foil and roast in a pre-heated oven at 180°C (350°F, Gas Mark 4) for about 40 minutes. Fold back the foil and increase the oven temperature to 220°C (425°F, Gas Mark 7) for a further 10 minutes to brown the skin.

Transfer to a carving plate and slice across in neat circles to serve. If you like a little sauce or glaze with your meat, pour the juices into a small roasting tin or pan, add the wine and 1 oz (25 g) butter and simmer for about 1 minute to thicken very slightly. Spoon over the turkey before serving.

Chicken Polo; Garlicky Turkey Drumstick

Rabbit and Rice Casserole

Serves 4

Preparation time: 40 minutes

Cooking time: 1½ hours

4 tablespoons oil

1 onion, chopped

1 clove garlic, crushed

3 sticks celery, chopped

8 oz (225 g) carrots, peeled and sliced

1½ lb (675 g) rabbit portions

½ pint (250 ml) chicken stock

½ pint (250 ml) dry white wine, cider or apple juice

salt and black pepper

1 teaspoon dry mustard powder

6 oz (150 g) American brown rice

1 teaspoon chopped parsley, to garnish

Heat half the oil in a pan and fry the onion and garlic until translucent. Add the celery and cook gently for 5 minutes. Transfer to a deep casserole with a tight-fitting lid, draining off as much fat as possible. Add the carrots to the casserole.

Add the rest of the oil to the pan and fry the rabbit portions until golden all over. Arrange these over the carrots in the casserole. Mix together the stock, wine, seasoning and mustard and pour over the rabbit. Finally, sprinkle on the rice, letting it fall down the casserole wherever possible and yet still form a top crust. Cover tightly and bake in a pre-heated oven at 180°C (350°F, Gas Mark 4) for 1½ hours. Give a gentle stir every 30 minutes, to shake the rice down the casserole, and, if necessary, add another ½ pint (250 ml) chicken stock 30 minutes before the end of cooking. Uncover the casserole for the last 10 minutes of the cooking time to allow the topping to crisp.

Serve sprinkled with the parsley.

Kidney Provençale

Serves 4
Preparation time: 35 minutes
Cooking time: 30 minutes

2 tablespoons oil
2 medium onions, chopped
12 oz (350 g) tomatoes, chopped
12 oz (350 g) kidneys, cored and chopped
$\frac{1}{3}$ pint (175 ml) beef stock
3 tablespoons sherry
a pinch each of oregano, thyme, sage and rosemary *or* 1 teaspooon dried mixed herbs
salt and pepper
6 oz (150 g) American long grain or brown rice, cooked as directed on page 7
1 oz (25 g) butter, melted
1 teaspoon chopped parsley, to garnish

Heat the oil in a large pan and gently fry the onions until translucent. Add the tomatoes and kidneys and cook over a high heat, stirring frequently, until the kidneys are no longer pink. Add the stock, sherry, herbs and seasoning to taste, and then simmer for another 15 minutes.

Serve the kidneys in a ring of hot, cooked rice to which the melted butter has been added. Sprinkle with parsley.

Rice 'n' Roast in a Pot

Serves 6—8
Preparation time: 20 minutes
Cooking time: 2 hours 40 minutes

1 tablespoon oil
1 large onion, sliced
2 sticks celery, chopped
2½ lb (1.25 kg) topside, silverside or blade of beef
2 tablespoons French mustard
8 oz (225 g) carrots, peeled and thickly sliced
8 oz (225 g) parsnips, peeled and thickly sliced
a few bay leaves
bouquet garni
1 pint (500 ml) beef stock
½ pint (250 ml) beer
8 oz (225 g) American long grain rice
1 tablespoon chopped parsley, to garnish

Heat the oil in a large pan and fry the onion and celery until translucent. Remove with a draining spoon and transfer to a heatproof casserole. Brown the meat on all sides in the oil, spread the mustard all over the beef and place the joint in the casserole. Surround it with the vegetables, add the bay leaves and bouquet garni, and pour on the stock and beer. Cover and cook in a pre-heated oven at 170°C (325°F, Gas Mark 3) for 2 hours, basting and stirring once.

Sprinkle on the rice, stir it into the liquid and cover tightly again. Increase the oven temperature to 200°C (400°F, Gas Mark 6) and cook for a further 40 minutes. Stir once or twice to distribute the rice in the stock.

To serve, remove and carve the beef, and sprinkle the rice with parsley.

Rice 'n' Roast in a Pot; Kidney Provençale;
Rabbit and Rice Casserole

Rice and Carrot Soufflé

Serves 4

Preparation time: 35 minutes

Cooking time: 40 minutes

1 lb (450 g) carrots, peeled and roughly chopped

1 large onion, quartered

1 large parsnip, peeled and roughly chopped

3 tablespoons double cream

1 tablespoon fresh orange juice

1 tablespoon chopped parsley

2 eggs, separated

4 oz (100 g) American brown rice, cooked in chicken stock

salt and black pepper

freshly grated nutmeg

2 oz (50 g) Gruyère cheese, grated

a few slices of fresh orange and sprigs of watercress, to garnish

Simmer the carrots, onion and parsnip in salted water until they are very tender. Drain and purée well or blend in a processor with the cream, orange juice, parsley and egg yolks. Then stir in the rice, seasoning and nutmeg to taste. Whisk the egg whites until stiff, fold them into the rice mixture and then spoon the mixture into a lightly greased 2 pint (1 litre) pudding basin. Sprinkle with the cheese and bake in a pre-heated oven at 180°C (350°F, Gas Mark 4) for about 40 minutes or until well risen, just firm to the touch and golden on top. Serve immediately, garnished with fresh orange slices and sprigs of watercress.

Fried Rice Cake with Parsley Sauce

Serves 4

Preparation time: 20 minutes

Cooking time: 28 minutes

Ⓕ Ⓥ

To make a non-vegetarian, family version of this dish, add a 7 oz (200 g) can of tuna, drained and flaked, or 8 oz (225 g) chopped bacon or chopped left-over roast meats.

1 lb (450 g) cooked American long grain rice

6 tablespoons sweetcorn kernels

6 tablespoons peas

1 small onion, finely chopped

salt and pepper

1 teaspoon dried mixed herbs

2 eggs, beaten

2 tablespoons oil

1 oz (25 g) butter or margarine

PARSLEY SAUCE:

$\frac{1}{2}$ oz (15 g) cornflour

$\frac{1}{2}$ oz (15 g) butter or margarine

7 fl oz (200 ml) milk

2 tablespoons chopped parsley

Mix together thoroughly the rice, sweetcorn, peas, onion, seasoning, herbs and eggs. Heat the oil and butter in a 7 inch (18 cm) non-stick frying pan with lid, and, when it is just bubbling, spoon in the rice mixture and press well down to form a neat, flat cake. Cook over a high heat for 3–4 minutes and then reduce the heat to cook very gently for a further 10 minutes. Carefully invert it on to a plate, slide it back into the pan and cook, as above, on the other side. Cut into quarters and serve with the parsley sauce.

To make the parsley sauce, whisk all the ingredients together in a small pan over a gentle heat until the sauce comes to the boil. Keep whisking or stirring with a wooden spoon for 3–4 minutes until cooked through and thickened slightly. Season to taste.

Risotto alla Milanese

Serves 4

Preparation time: 10 minutes

Cooking time: 30 minutes

A risotto is usually a meal in itself, the rice tacky and deliciously tasty after the long, slow cooking. This one is ideal for vegetarians. Or, for a family meal, serve it with veal or pork chops cooked in tomato sauce, fried and sliced spicy or garlic sausages, poached or roast chicken portions, or cold roast meats.

1 onion, chopped
2 oz (50 g) butter
8 oz (225 g) American long grain rice
1½ pints (750 ml) boiling chicken or vegetable stock
1 glass dry white wine
1 teaspoon turmeric powder
1 oz (25 g) grated Parmesan cheese
1 teaspoon chopped parsley, to garnish

Fry the onion in half the butter until translucent. Add the rice and toss over a high heat for 1 minute. Add the stock, 2–3 tablespoons wine and the turmeric and mix well. Bring back to the boil, cover tightly and simmer very slowly for about 30 minutes, stirring occasionally.

After 30 minutes, add the rest of the wine, the rest of the butter and the cheese. Mix well and serve immediately, sprinkled with the parsley. (This type of rice takes well to being served in a pretty shape, see page 10.)

Risotto alla Milanese; Fried Rice Cake with
Parsley Sauce; Rice and Carrot Soufflé

Celery, Rice and Chilli Bean Bake

Serves 4

Preparation time: 40 minutes

Cooking time: 35 minutes

14 oz (400 g) can red kidney beans, drained

1 small onion, chopped

1 teaspoon chilli powder

1 teaspoon lemon juice

1 teaspoon chopped fresh parsley *or* $\frac{1}{2}$ teaspoon dried parsley

$\frac{1}{2}$ × $10\frac{1}{2}$ oz (295 g) can condensed cream of celery soup

$\frac{1}{4}$ pint (125 ml) chicken stock

12 oz (350 g) cooked American brown rice

2 oz (50 g) brown breadcrumbs

2 oz (50 g) Cheddar cheese, grated

a little chopped celery leaf or parsley, to garnish

Mix together the beans, onion, chilli powder, lemon juice and
parsley. Mix together the soup, stock and rice. Layer these two
alternately in an ovenproof dish, ending with rice. Top with a thick
layer of breadcrumbs and cheese mixed together. Bake in a pre-
heated oven at 200°C (400°F, Gas Mark 6) for about 35 minutes, or
until bubbling and golden on top. Sprinkle with chopped celery
leaves or parsley before serving.

Rice and Vegetable Fritters

Serves 4 (Makes at least 12 fritters)

Preparation time: 45 minutes

Cooking time: 20 minutes

Ⓕ (uncooked) Ⓥ

For a family snack, these are very good made with finely chopped left-over roast meat, or bacon, instead of the vegetables.

2 eggs, lightly beaten

2 oz (50 g) plain flour

pepper

onion salt

2 oz (50 g) peas

2 oz (50 g) sweetcorn kernels

4 oz (100 g) cooked American brown rice

oil, for frying

1 tablespoon grated Parmesan cheese

Beat together the eggs and flour until quite smooth. Add the seasoning, vegetables and rice.

Heat the oil in a non-stick frying pan and drop in tablespoons of the fritter mixture. Cook only four or five at a time, for 3 minutes on each side, or until golden and crispy. Drain on kitchen paper and sprinkle with cheese just before serving.

Chinese Fried Rice

Serves 4

Preparation time: 10 minutes

Cooking time: 10 minutes

This is an excellent way to use up left-over rice, and other ingredients, to serve either as an accompaniment or as a supper dish. Many variations can be made by adding meat, chicken, shrimps, other fish or vegetables.

2 tablespoons vegetable oil

2 eggs, lightly beaten

14—16 oz (400—450 g) cooked American long grain rice

8 spring onions, chopped

4 oz (100 g) cooked pork or other meat, finely chopped, or prawns

4 oz (100 g) left-over vegetables, e.g. peas, carrots or sweetcorn

salt and pepper

1 tablespoon chicken stock

Heat the oil in a wok or light-weight frying pan. Add the beaten egg and stir-fry or toss rapidly with a fork until set but not browned. Add the rice, onions, meat or prawns and vegetables. Toss over a high heat for 2—3 minutes. Add seasoning to taste and the stock to moisten, and serve immediately.

Rice and Vegetable Fritters; Celery, Rice and Chilli Bean Bake; Chinese Fried Rice

Baked Aubergine with Olives

Serves 4

Preparation time: 40 minutes

Cooking time: 1 hour

Ⓕ Ⓥ

Using olive oil and the big, juicy black olives, this dish has a warm Mediterranean taste and rich olive aroma. Even if you don't like anchovies, try them in this recipe: you won't taste them specifically but they do make all the difference to the final flavour.

2 aubergines of equal size and even shape
4 tablespoons olive oil
1 onion, chopped
1 clove garlic, crushed
4 tomatoes, chopped
6–7 anchovy fillets, drained
1 teaspoon chopped fresh basil *or* ½ teaspoon dried basil
1 tablespoon chopped fresh parsley *or* 1 teaspoon dried parsley
salt and pepper
5–6 large, soft, black olives, stoned and sliced
12 oz (350 g) cooked American brown rice
5 oz (125 g) Mozzarella cheese, thinly sliced

Cut the ends off the aubergines and cut both in half lengthways. Trim the bases so that they are flat. Scoop out the centres to leave firm shells, and brush these with oil. Chop the aubergine flesh, sprinkle with salt and place on a plate for 10 minutes.

Heat the rest of the oil and fry the onion and garlic until translucent. Add the tomatoes, anchovy fillets and herbs. Drain and rinse the aubergine flesh and add to the pan. Cook gently, stirring frequently, for about 5 minutes or until well mixed and slightly softened. Season to taste. Add the olive flesh and the rice.

Pack this mixture into the aubergine shells. Top with the sliced cheese. Wrap each portion in a foil case, place on a baking tray and bake in a pre-heated oven at 180°C (350°F, Gas Mark 4) for about 1 hour. Just before serving, fold back the foil and brown the cheese under the grill if you wish.

Bacon and Mushroom Casserole with Rice Dumplings

Serves 4
Preparation time: 20 minutes
Cooking time: 50 minutes

1 tablespoon vegetable oil
1 large onion, sliced
1 lb (450 g) boiling bacon or gammon (soaked in cold water for 4 hours)
10½ oz (295 g) can of condensed mushroom soup
½ pint (250 ml) apple juice
¼ pint (125 ml) chicken stock
1 teaspoon dried oregano
2–3 bay leaves
1 red-skinned apple, cored and chopped
4 oz (100 g) mushrooms, sliced

RICE DUMPLINGS:

6 oz (150 g) American brown rice, cooked as directed on page 7
1 oz (25 g) plain flour
1 tablespoon mustard powder
salt and pepper
a few chives, chopped, to garnish

Heat the oil in a large saucepan or ovenproof casserole dish and fry the onion until translucent. Then add the bacon or gammon, the soup, the apple juice, stock, oregano and bay leaves. Bring to the boil and simmer gently for 30 minutes or until the bacon is cooked. Add the apple and mushrooms.

Mix together the freshly cooked rice, flour, mustard and seasoning. Shape into 10–12 small balls and place these on top of the casserole. Cover and return to the oven for a further 20 minutes.

When the dumplings have swollen and are crispy on top, serve the casserole sprinkled with the chives.

Cheese Galantine with Cocktail Sauce

Serves 4—6

Preparation time: 20 minutes

Chilling time: 1 hour

3 oz (75 g) American long grain rice, cooked as directed on page 7

6 oz (150 g) cottage cheese

2 oz (50 g) Mozzarella cheese, grated

1 tomato, skinned and chopped

2 spring onions, white only, chopped

1 teaspoon sesame seeds

1 teaspoon chopped parsley

salt and black pepper

COCKTAIL SAUCE:

3 tablespoons mayonnaise

1 tablespoon milk

1 teaspoon tomato purée

a few drops Worcestershire sauce or chilli sauce

1 teaspoon lemon juice

2—3 black olives and 1 gherkin fan, to garnish

It is important to use the rice in this recipe while it is still hot. Mix it with the cottage cheese, Mozzarella cheese, tomato, onions, sesame seeds, parsley and seasoning. When well blended, pack into a clingfilm-lined 1 pint (0.5 litre) pâté dish or mould. Chill for 1 hour.

For the sauce, blend together all the ingredients until smooth. Chill until required.

Turn out the galantine and serve with the sauce poured over and garnished with slices of olive and the gherkin fan in the centre.

Bacon and Mushroom Casserole with Rice Dumplings;
Cheese Galantine with Cocktail Sauce;
Baked Aubergine with Olives

Liver and Bacon Pudding

Serves 4

Preparation time: 40 minutes

Cooking time: 55 minutes

a little butter or margarine

2 oz (50 g) fresh brown breadcrumbs

8 oz (225 g) streaky bacon, de-rinded and chopped

8 oz (225 g) lamb's or pig's liver, chopped

1 small onion, chopped

1 teaspoon lemon juice

10 oz (275 g) cooked American brown rice

1 teaspoon dried parsley

$\frac{1}{2}$ teaspoon dried, rubbed sage

1 egg, beaten

$\frac{1}{4}$ pint (125 ml) lamb or beef stock

salt and pepper

4 grilled bacon rolls and a few fresh sage or watercress leaves, to garnish

Well-butter a 2 pint (1 litre) pudding basin and press the crumbs into this butter to give a good coating. Mix together the bacon, liver, onion, lemon juice, rice and herbs. Beat together the egg and stock and blend into the rice mixture. Season to taste. Pack into the pudding basin, cover tightly with foil or greaseproof paper and steam for 45 minutes.

Turn out carefully on to an ovenproof serving plate and brown off in a pre-heated oven at 220°C (425°F, Gas Mark 7) for 10 minutes. Garnish with the bacon rolls and sage or watercress leaves. Serve with gravy or a hot tomato sauce and vegetables.

Cheese Milanese Crunchies

Serves 4

Preparation time: 20 minutes (plus chilling time)

Cooking time: 15 minutes

Ⓕ Ⓥ

This delicious recipe is best using left-over Risotto alla Milanese (see page 24). However, any cooked left-over rice can be used, and the stickier it is, the better! So if you still haven't got your rice cooking to perfection, here's the perfect way to use up your failures!

1 lb (450 g) left-over risotto or cooked American short grain rice

1 egg, beaten

6 oz (150 g) Bel Paese or Mozzarella cheese

seasoning: if you use risotto you will need little or no seasoning; if you use left-over plain rice add salt and pepper to taste, a little garlic salt or garlic paste, and 1 tablespoon chopped fresh mixed herbs *or* 1 teaspoon dried mixed herbs

4 oz (100 g) fresh white breadcrumbs

oil, for frying

1 tablespoon grated Parmesan cheese

Mix together the rice, beaten egg and 3 oz (75 g) of the Bel Paese or Mozzarella cheese, grated. Season according to the rice you are using. Divide the remaining cheese into 12 small cubes. Take a dessertspoonful of the mixture, put a cube of cheese in the middle and top with a little more rice. Put this into a bowl containing the breadcrumbs and gently coat very well with crumbs and shape into a ball. (It's a very messy job but very well worth it!) Repeat with the remaining rice mixture and cheese cubes.

Leave the cheese balls to chill for at least 2 hours, or overnight. Place 3 or 4 at a time in deep, hot fat carefully and turn them immediately to seal them. Cook for about 5 minutes each, turning once more to brown them evenly. Remove and drain on kitchen paper, then toss in Parmesan cheese. Eat as soon as possible.

Eggs in Florentine Nests

Serves 4

Preparation time: 45 minutes

Cooking time: 32 minutes

Ⓕ Ⓥ

This recipe is equally good with either freshly cooked or left-over rice. Add any other left-over vegetables you may have; you could, in fact, leave out the eggs and add extra vegetables if you prefer.

1 lb (450 g) frozen, chopped spinach, thawed
6 oz (150 g) American brown rice, cooked as directed on page 7
salt and pepper
a little oil
4 eggs
$\frac{1}{2}$ pint (250 ml) milk
$\frac{1}{4}$ pint (125 ml) vegetable, herb or chicken stock
$\frac{3}{4}$ oz (20 g) cornflour
$\frac{1}{2}$ oz (15 g) butter
4 oz (100 g) Cheddar cheese, grated

Carefully drain the spinach of any excess liquid and mix with the rice and seasoning to taste. Lightly oil an ovenproof dish and spread the rice mixture evenly in the base. Make four slight hollows in the rice and crack one egg into each hollow.

Whisk together the milk, stock and cornflour. Heat the butter in a pan and whisk in the liquid. Bring slowly to the boil, whisking occasionally, and then cook for 2 minutes, stirring all the time. Stir in three-quarters of the cheese, off the heat. Season to taste and then spoon over the rice and eggs. Sprinkle with the remaining cheese and bake in a pre-heated oven at 180°C (350°F, Gas Mark 4) for about 30 minutes. Brown the top under a hot grill for 1–2 minutes if you wish.

Eggs in Florentine Nests; Liver and Bacon Pudding;
Cheese Milanese Crunchies

Jambalaya

Serves 4

Preparation time: 20 minutes

Cooking time: about 1 hour

As the name implies, this is a delicious 'jumble' of ingredients. It originated in colourful New Orleans, so the dish should be as colourful as possible too, and slightly hot and spicy. Use left-over ingredients as you wish.

1 large onion
1 red pepper, de-seeded
1 green pepper, de-seeded
2 sticks celery
4 large tomatoes, skinned
12 oz (350 g) American long grain rice
2 pints (1 litre) boiling chicken stock
1 teaspoon dried basil
1 teaspoon dried thyme
10—12 oz (275—350 g) cooked meat or fish, chopped or flaked
$\frac{1}{2}$—1 teaspoon Tabasco sauce
salt and pepper
2 tablespoons chopped parsley, to garnish

Finely chop all the vegetables and put them in a large pan with the rice, stock and herbs. Bring back to the boil, cover tightly and simmer gently for about 1 hour, stirring occasionally. Add the meat or fish, Tabasco sauce and then seasoning to taste. Finally, sprinkle with parsley and serve.

Rice Salads

American rice can make many delicious salads which are economical for entertaining large numbers, and which will keep very well for 2—3 days in the fridge. In fact, the flavour often improves on keeping. Be sure not to overcook the rice—it should still be nutty—otherwise with the addition of a dressing it can lose its crunchiness. You will get the best results by mixing the freshly cooked rice with the particular dressing you are using immediately. This way the grains absorb the maximum flavour. Cool and then mix in the other ingredients as required. If you are using mayonnaise, allow the rice to cool slightly before you mix it in. Most rice salads do freeze, but you may need to add extra flavour or dressing after thawing. Rice salads can be served hot too. Here are some interesting and tasty combinations to add to 12 oz (350 g) cooked American long grain white or brown rice (4 oz (100 g) uncooked American rice) which will serve four people as an accompanying salad.

☆ 7—8 tablespoons french dressing; 2 sticks celery, chopped; 1 crisp apple, cored and chopped; $\frac{1}{2}$ oz (15 g) salted peanuts to sprinkle on top.

☆ $\frac{1}{4}$ pint (125 ml) blue cheese dressing; 4 oz (100 g) tiny cauliflower florets, blanched; 1 green pepper, de-seeded and chopped; 1 small avocado, chopped.

☆ 7—8 tablespoons french dressing flavoured with $\frac{1}{2}$ teaspoon grated orange rind; 1 orange, segmented; 6 oz (150 g) cooked chicken, chopped; 2 oz (50 g) white bread, cut in cubes and fried in garlic-flavoured oil; 6 spring onions, chopped, with the green tops.

☆ $\frac{1}{4}$ pint (125 ml) mustard dressing made from 5 tablespoons natural yogurt, 5 tablespoons french dressing, and 1 tablespoon chive mustard; 1 onion, finely chopped; 4 oz (100 g) cooked sweetcorn kernels; 4 oz (100 g) cooked green beans; 1 tablespoon chopped chives to sprinkle on top.

☆ $\frac{1}{4}$ pint (125 ml) creamy mayonnaise and 1 tablespoon lemon juice; $4\frac{1}{2}$ oz (137 g) can tuna, drained and flaked; 2 oz (50 g) stoned black olives, chopped; 2 tablespoons chopped parsley; lemon wedges, to serve.

(Rice Salads are illustrated on the title page.)

Stuffings

Rice makes the perfect stuffing base for poultry and other joints. But you don't have to use a stuffing, as it's name implies, inside meat. Pack it into a small tin, brush with dripping or lard and bake it with the roast. In the Southern United States, stuffings are called 'dressings' and are usually served as a main or side dish.

Quantities given will serve 6, or make enough to stuff a 4 lb (2 kg) chicken.

Rice Stuffing

1 onion, sliced

gizzard and liver of 1 chicken, minced or finely chopped

2 sticks celery, minced

1 green pepper, de-seeded and minced

pepper

1—2 teaspoons Tabasco sauce

oil, lard or dripping

1 lb (4500 g) American long grain rice, cooked as directed on page 7

Fry all the ingredients except the rice in the fat, with seasoning to taste and 2—3 tablespoons water, for 10—15 minutes. Mix in the cooked rice and serve.

Fruit and Nut Stuffing

12 oz (350 g) American long grain rice, cooked as directed on page 7

1 onion, finely chopped

4 oz (100 g) dates, chopped

2 oz (50 g) California seedless raisins

2 oz (50 g) USA pecan nuts, chopped

2 oz (50 g) salted peanuts

salt and pepper

Make sure the rice is only just cooked and still slightly nutty. Mix together all the ingredients thoroughly, while either hot or cold. Season to taste.

Slightly Spiced Stuffing

12 oz (350 g) American brown rice, cooked as directed on page 7

4 oz (100 g) mushrooms, finely chopped

4 oz (100 g) sweetcorn kernels

2 tomatoes, peeled and chopped

1 teaspoon curry powder

1 teaspoon cumin seeds

1 teaspoon mustard seeds, crushed

$\frac{1}{2}$ teaspoon crushed black peppercorns

salt

Mix together all the ingredients and season to taste.

Spicy Apple Dumplings

Serves 5–6

Preparation time: 1 hour

Cooking time: 10 minutes

Use left-over cooked rice pudding for this delicious pudding, or cook 3 oz (75 g) American short grain rice in 1 pint (500 ml) milk, with sugar to taste, until the rice is cooked, but still very sticky.

10 oz (275 g) left-over cooked rice pudding, chilled

1 small apple, peeled and cut into 10–12 thick slices

2 oz (50 g) brown breadcrumbs

1 oz (25 g) soft dark brown sugar

$\frac{1}{4}$ teaspoon mixed spice

1 egg, beaten

oil and butter or margarine, for frying

apple sauce, to serve

Mould 10–12 spoonfuls of rice around the slices of apple. Shape neatly so that the apple is well sealed in. Mix together the crumbs, sugar and mixed spice. Coat the rice balls in egg and then the spiced crumbs, pressing them on well to give a good, thick coating. Heat about $\frac{1}{4}$ inch (5 mm) fat and carefully fry all the dumplings together for about 5 minutes, turning them once or twice so that they become crisp all over. Drain on kitchen paper before serving with apple sauce.

Tutti Fruiti Rice Meringue

Serves 4—5
Preparation time: 55 minutes
Cooking time: 20 minutes

This pudding can be made with either left-over cooked rice pudding or freshly cooked rice.

4 oz (100 g) American short grain rice, cooked as directed on page 7, *or* 12 oz (350 g) left-over rice pudding
white or brown sugar, to taste
2 oz (50 g) chopped ready-to-eat apricots
2 oz (50 g) California seedless raisins
1 teaspoon finely grated orange rind
1 teaspoon finely grated lemon rind
2 egg whites
3 oz (75 g) caster sugar
1 tablespoon toasted sesame seeds

Mix the cooked rice with sugar to taste, the dried fruits and the fruit rinds. Spoon into an ovenproof serving dish. Whisk the egg whites until stiff and fold in the sugar and most of the sesame seeds. Spoon the meringue over the rice pudding and sprinkle the rest of the seeds on top. Bake in a pre-heated oven at 180°C (350°F, Gas Mark 4) for 15—20 minutes or until the top is golden brown.

Tutti Fruiti Rice Meringue; Spicy Apple Dumplings

Apricot Rice Ring

Serves 6–8

Preparation time: 50 minutes (plus chilling time)

4 oz (100 g) American short grain rice

$1\frac{1}{2}$ pints (750 ml) milk

a few drops vanilla essence

1 sachet (3 teaspoons) gelatine

$14\frac{1}{2}$ oz (411 g) can apricot halves in syrup

4 tablespoons apricot jam

2 oz (50 g) creamed coconut, grated

2 egg whites

Gently simmer the rice in the milk, stirring occasionally, for about 30 minutes or until soft and creamy. Then stir in a few drops of vanilla essence and the gelatine powder. Leave to stand for 5 minutes while the gelatine dissolves. Add the apricot syrup and 5–6 apricot halves. Reserve the rest for the centre of the ring.

With an electric whisk, or in a food processor, blend the rice, fruit, jam and $1\frac{1}{2}$ oz (40 g) coconut for about 5 minutes, until smoothish. Whisk the egg whites until stiff and fold into the rice pudding. Line a 2 pint (1 litre) sponge flan tin with clingfilm and fill with the rice. Chill for about 2 hours.

Turn out on to a plate and fill the centre with the remaining apricot halves. Sprinkle with the rest of the grated coconut.

Coffee Flan with Banana and Nut Topping

Serves 4—6

Preparation time: 55 minutes (plus chilling time)

4 oz (100 g) American short grain rice

$\frac{1}{2}$ pint (250 ml) milk

$\frac{1}{2}$ pint (250 ml) black coffee

soft brown sugar, to taste

$\frac{1}{2}$ sachet (1$\frac{1}{2}$ teaspoons) gelatine

$\frac{1}{4}$ pint (125 ml) double or whipping cream

2 egg whites

1 banana, sliced and dipped in lemon juice

2 oz (50 g) flaked almonds, toasted

Put the rice in a heavy, non-stick saucepan with the milk, coffee and sugar and bring to the boil. Cover tightly and simmer very slowly for about 30 minutes, until the rice is tender and all the liquid has been absorbed. Stir frequently during cooking and if it seems to be sticking badly, add a little extra milk. When cooked, sprinkle on the gelatine, stir for a few minutes to allow the gelatine to dissolve and then leave the rice to cool.

Whip the cream and stiffly whisk the egg whites. When the rice is cool but not set, fold in the cream and egg whites and spoon into a 2 pint (1 litre) sponge flan tin, lined with clingfilm for easy removal, if you wish. Chill for 2 hours.

Turn out on to a plate and arrange the banana slices around the edge. Sprinkle the nuts in the centre.

Chilled Chocolate and Pear Slice

Serves 6

Preparation time: 15 minutes (plus chilling time)

4 oz (100 g) dark chocolate

1 tablespoon golden syrup

8 oz (225 g) left-over rice pudding or sweet cooked rice

4 oz (100 g) California seedless raisins

4 oz (100 g) digestive biscuits, crushed

2 pears, peeled, cored and sliced

a little whipped cream

Melt the chocolate and syrup together and then mix in the rice pudding, raisins and biscuits. When well mixed, pack the mixture into a 7—8 inch (18—20 cm) flan or sponge tin, lined with clingfilm. Chill for several hours. (This mixture will never set really hard, but will become firm enough to slice.)

Turn out on to a serving plate and top with the sliced pears and decorate with a little whipped cream.

Apricot Rice Ring; Chilled Chocolate and Pear Slice;
Coffee Flan with Banana and Nut Topping

Kids' Corner

Feeding children, especially if they are eating different meals at very different times from the adults in the house, can be a nightmare, so here are some new ideas to help you and to tempt the younger appetites. For older and more responsible children who are beginning to take an interest in cooking, there are several easy dishes which they may like to cook themselves, the Curried Frankfurter Salad for instance, the Ham Riceburgers, the sweets or the Stuffed Apple Meringues. And as so many people have packed lunches these days, you will find portable ideas suitable for picnics or school lunches.

Sausage and Cheese Bake

Serves 4

Preparation time: 30 minutes

Cooking time: 15 minutes

8 oz (225 g) beef sausages

½ pint (250 ml) white sauce

12 oz (350 g) cooked American long grain rice

4 oz (100 g) Cheddar cheese, grated

1 tablespoon chopped chives

2 tablespoons peas

salt and pepper

1 packet plain crisps

Grill the sausages until well browned all over and cooked through. Cool slightly and then thinly slice them. Mix the hot sauce with the rice, cheese, chives and peas. Season to taste. Layer the sausages and rice mixture in an ovenproof dish, ending with a rice layer. Roughly crush the crisps with your hands and sprinkle over the top. Bake in a pre-heated oven at 190°C (375°F, Gas Mark 5) for about 15 minutes.

Rice Fish Cakes

Makes 8—10 cakes
Preparation time: 45 minutes
Cooking time: 10 minutes

It is quite easy to shape this mixture into cakes, but if your family are fish finger freaks, you may want to try making it into fingers! If you do, chill the mixture well before cooking so that the fingers remain nicely shaped.

3 oz (75 g) American brown rice, cooked as directed on page 7
8 oz (225 g) haddock, skinned, boned, poached and flaked
1 egg
1 tablespoon flour
1 teaspoon lemon juice
salt, pepper and grated nutmeg
1 teaspoon chopped parsley
2 oz (50 g) brown breadcrumbs
oil and butter or margarine mixed, for frying

Put the rice into a mixing bowl and mix in the flaked fish, egg, flour, lemon juice, seasoning to taste and parsley. Knead the mixture well together until it feels sticky. Divide and shape into 8—10 flat cakes. Coat the fish cakes well in breadcrumbs, pressing them in. (A double coating does give a better-looking result but there really is no need.) Chill until required and then fry in about $\frac{1}{2}$ inch (1 cm) fat until crisp and golden. This will take about 5 minutes each side. Drain on kitchen paper and serve immediately.

Corn Chowder

Serves 4

Preparation time: 20 minutes

Cooking time: 35 minutes

This is a fairly substantial soup which is ideal as a main supper dish, perhaps just with granary bread, and some fruit to follow.

2 oz (50 g) American long grain rice

1 pint (500 ml) boiling chicken stock

5 oz (125 g) sweetcorn kernels

¼ pint (125 ml) milk

2 tomatoes, chopped

1 tablespoon tomato purée

salt and pepper

4 rashers streaky bacon, de-rinded, grilled and chopped

1½ oz (40 g) Edam or Gouda cheese, grated

Place the rice in a large pan with the stock. Bring to the boil, cover and simmer gently for about 20 minutes. Then add the sweetcorn, milk, tomatoes, tomato purée and seasoning to taste. Simmer for a further 10—15 minutes. Add the bacon—which is best when it is quite crisp and crunchy—and pour the soup into individual heatproof dishes. Top with the grated cheese and pop the dishes under a hot grill for about 1 minute until the cheese has melted.

Sausage and Cheese Bake; Corn Chowder;
Rice Fish Cakes

Crispy Surprise Mince

Serves 4

Preparation time: 40 minutes

Cooking time: 1¼ hours

You can make this with any ingredients you may have handy
or left over.

1 tablespoon oil
1 onion, chopped
12 oz (350 g) lean minced beef
4 oz (100 g) American brown rice
1 pint (500 ml) beef stock
a few drops Worcestershire sauce
4 oz (100 g) mushrooms, sliced
6 oz (150 g) carrots, cooked and sliced
salt and pepper
2 tomatoes, sliced
2 oz (50 g) Cheddar cheese, grated
1 oz (25 g) granary breadcrumbs

In a large pan, heat the oil and fry the onion until translucent. Add
the mince and cook until browned all over. Add the rice and toss
over a high heat for 5 minutes. Add the stock and sauce and bring
to the boil.

Transfer to an ovenproof dish, cover tightly and cook in a pre-
heated oven at 180°C (350°F, Gas Mark 4) for about 1 hour. Stir
occasionally and add extra liquid if the mixture seems to be drying
out. Stir in the mushrooms, carrots and seasoning to taste. Cover
with a layer of sliced tomatoes, then with the cheese and crumbs
mixed together. Return to the oven and bake for a further 15
minutes at 200°C (400°F, Gas Mark 6) until the top is golden.

Curried Fish Plait

Serves 6

Preparation time: 40 minutes

Cooking time: 40 minutes

Ⓕ

7 oz (200 g) wholemeal shortcrust pastry

a little flour

6 oz (150 g) cooked American long grain or brown rice

2 tablespoons mild curry sauce or paste

1 teaspoon tomato sauce

8 oz (225 g) smoked cod, haddock or kipper

2 small tomatoes, sliced

1 small egg, beaten

Roll out the pastry on a floured surface to a rectangle approximately 10 inches × 8 inches (25 cm × 20 cm). Mix the rice, curry sauce, tomato sauce and fish together and spread the mixture on the middle of the pastry, leaving 3 inches (7.5 cm) pastry on either side and 1 inch (2.5 cm) at each end. Arrange the sliced tomatoes over the fish.

Make diagonal slits in the sides of the pastry, $\frac{1}{2}$ inch (1 cm) apart, from the edge into the filling. Brush the pastry with beaten egg. Fold over the top and bottom ends, then take strips of dough from alternate sides into the centre, so that they just meet or overlap, in a plait or braid design. Seal the ends well. Brush the pastry all over with egg and place the plait on a baking sheet. Bake in a pre-heated oven at 190°C (375°F, Gas Mark 5) for 35–40 minutes, or until the pastry is crisp and golden. Serve hot or cold.

Bacon Crispies

Serves 6—8

Preparation time: 25 minutes

Cooking time: 40 minutes

Ⓕ (without the crispy base as it would go soft)

4 skinless sausages, grilled

8 rashers streaky bacon, de-rinded and grilled

2 eggs

½ pint (250 ml) milk

6 oz (150 g) cooked American long grain or brown rice

seasoning (optional)

6 oz (150 g) plain, salted crisps

2 oz (50 g) rolled oats

4 oz (100 g) butter or margarine, melted

Thinly slice the sausages and chop the bacon. Lay them in the bottom of a lightly greased, shallow, rectangular baking tin, approximately 12 inches × 8 inches (30 cm × 20 cm). Beat the eggs, milk and rice together and season if you wish (remembering the salt in the crisps, bacon and sausages!). Pour evenly over the sausages and bacon and cook in a pre-heated oven at 180°C (350°F, Gas Mark 4) for about 20 minutes.

Lightly crush the crisps, mix with the oats and toss in the melted butter or margarine. When well mixed, spread over the egg mixture and press it in lightly to give an even surface. Return to the oven for a further 20 minutes.

To serve, loosen the edges slightly, then invert the tin on to a rectangular plate or board, so that the crisps form the base. Cut into squares or fingers immediately and serve hot or cold.

Bacon Crispies; Crispy Surprise Mince; Curried Fish Plait

Curried Frankfurter Salad

Serves 4

Preparation time: 1½ hours

This dish is great fun to prepare and it can look so exciting, especially if the younger members of the family do it!

6 oz (150 g) American long grain rice, cooked as directed on page 7
1 teaspoon curry powder
1 tablespoon vegetable oil
1 tablespoon orange juice
3 tablespoons natural yogurt
2 oz (50 g) California seedless raisins
½ red pepper, chopped
½ green pepper, chopped
salt and pepper
8 small Frankfurter sausages *or* 4 large ones, halved
2 oz (50 g) dry roasted peanuts
2 poppadums, cooked and roughly crushed, *or* 1 packet of corn chips, to garnish

As soon as the rice is cooked, stir in the curry powder, oil, orange juice and yogurt. Make sure you coat all the rice well with the liquids first, and then stir in the raisins, peppers and season to taste.

Cook or heat through the Frankfurters, slice them and add them to the rice with the peanuts. Garnish with the poppadums or corn chips, and serve with a selection of chutneys or relishes.

Rice Castles with Bolognese Sauce

Serves 4
Preparation time: 20 minutes
Cooking time: 20 minutes

This is a great way to serve rice to kids, topped off with flags, or pieces of cheese, celery or carrot. In fact, younger children would probably enjoy helping you prepare these rice castles.

1 onion, chopped
2 carrots, finely chopped
1 stick celery, finely chopped
1 tablespoon oil
8 oz (225 g) minced beef
8 oz (225 g) can tomatoes
¼ pint (125 ml) beef stock
6 oz (150 g) American long grain rice, cooked as directed on page 7
salt and pepper
1 tablespoon chopped chives or parsley
a knob of butter

Fry the finely chopped vegetables in oil for 1–2 minutes until translucent. Add the beef and toss until browned. Add the tomatoes and stock, cover and then simmer gently for about 20 minutes, or until the sauce is thickened.

Season the hot rice to taste and stir in the chives or parsley and butter. Divide the rice between four small moulds (or small cups would do) and pack well in. Leave for 5 minutes, then invert on to individual plates, pour the Bolognese sauce around the rice and add any finishing touches, as suggested above, if you wish.

Ham Riceburgers

Makes 8

Preparation time: 20 minutes (plus chilling time)

Cooking time: 15 minutes

12 oz (350 g) gammon or boiling bacon, minced

12 oz (350 g) cooked American long grain rice

2 spring onions, finely chopped

1 egg, beaten

1 oz (25 g) breadcrumbs

oil, for frying

Mix together the ham, rice and chopped onions until well mixed. Divide the mixture into eight portions and shape into flat cakes or burgers. Dip first into beaten egg and then the breadcrumbs to give a good, even coating. Chill for 30 minutes or more.

Fry in a little hot oil for 2 minutes quickly on each side to brown, and then for 5 minutes slowly each side to cook through.

Drain on kitchen paper. Serve with a fresh tomato or barbecue sauce or baked beans.

Curried Frankfurter Salad; Ham Riceburgers;
Rice Castles with Bolognese Sauce

Orange Rice-cream

Serves 6—8 (Makes 1½ pints (750 ml))

Preparation time: 3—3½ hours

Freezing time: 8—10 hours

4 oz (100 g) American short grain rice

1 pint (500 ml) milk

4 tablespoons clear honey

4 tablespoons frozen concentrated orange juice

finely grated rind and flesh of 1 orange

a few drops vanilla essence

½ pint (250 ml) single cream

4 oz (100 g) California seedless raisins

Cook the rice slowly in the milk in a heavy saucepan as directed on page 7 for about 30 minutes, until the rice is very soft. Allow to cool. Add the honey, orange juice, orange rind and flesh, a few drops of vanilla essence, and the cream. Either beat very thoroughly for 3—4 minutes with an electric whisk, or blend in a processor for 1 minute. Transfer to a freezing container and part-freeze for 2—3 hours.

When firm but not frozen, whisk for a minute or so lightly and then stir in the raisins. Freeze until quite firm. Allow 20 minutes thawing time to soften before serving.

Pineapple Surprise

Serves 4
Preparation time: 30 minutes (plus chilling time)
Cooking time: 25 minutes

4 oz (100 g) American short grain rice
1 pint (500 ml) milk
2 oz (50 g) marshmallows, chopped
7 oz (200 g) can pineapple rings
1 packet mandarin jelly
angelica, to decorate
mandarin yogurt, to serve

Cook the rice in the milk as directed on page 7 for only about 35 minutes. Add the marshmallows. Reserve three rings of pineapple; drain the rest and dry them on kitchen paper. Chop them and add them to the rice.

Dissolve the jelly in only $\frac{1}{4}$ pint (125 ml) water. Keep back 3 tablespoons and add the rest to the warm rice. Add a further 3 tablespoons of water to the remaining jelly and pour this into the base of a 2 pint (1 litre) jelly mould or tin. Arrange the three slices of pineapple in this and leave to set. Spoon in the rice filling and then chill for 2—3 hours.

Dip the mould or tin into boiling water for a few seconds and then carefully turn the jelly out on to a serving dish. Decorate with pieces of angelica and serve with mandarin yogurt.

Stuffed Apple Meringues

Serves 4
Preparation time: 20 minutes
Cooking time: 1 hour 40 minutes

2 oz (50 g) American brown rice
⅓ pint (175 ml) milk
soft brown sugar, to taste
1 oz (25 g) California seedless raisins
1 teaspoon mixed spice
4 cooking apples
2 egg whites
4 oz (100 g) caster sugar

Cook the rice in the milk as directed on page 7 for about 40 minutes or until it is very tender and all the liquid has been absorbed. Add brown sugar to taste, the raisins and the spices. Peel and core the cooking apples, taking out sufficient apple to make room for the filling. Place the apples on a baking tray or flat ovenproof dish. Divide the filling evenly between the apples.

Whisk the egg whites until stiff, and then gently whisk in half the sugar. Gradually fold in the rest of the sugar and spoon the meringue mixture all over and around the apples. Bake in a pre-heated oven at 180°C (350°F, Gas Mark 4) for about 1 hour, when the meringue should be nicely golden.

Pineapple Surprise; Orange Rice-cream;
Stuffed Apple Meringues

Date Slices

Makes 10 slices

Preparation time: 15 minutes

Cooking time: 40 minutes

These slices make a lovely, gooey snack, ideal for school lunches or picnics.

4 oz (100 g) wholewheat flour

4 oz (100 g) margarine

$\frac{1}{2}$ teaspoon baking powder

2 oz (50 g) rolled oats

1 tablespoon brown sugar

6 oz (150 g) cooked American brown rice

8 oz (225 g) pitted dates, chopped

2 tablespoons clear honey

1 tablespoon lemon juice

Rub the flour and margarine together until they resemble fine breadcrumbs. Stir in the baking powder, oats, sugar, rice and dates until really well mixed. Bind the mixture together with the honey and lemon juice to give a stiff consistency. Press into a 7—8 inch (18—20 cm) square tin and bake in a pre-heated oven at 190°C (375°F, Gas Mark 5) for 40 minutes, or until golden and slightly crispy on top. Cut into slices or wedges immediately and then leave to cool before removing from the tin.

Yellow Rice Cakes with Fruity Sauce

Serves 4
Preparation time: $1\frac{1}{4}$ hours

3 oz (75 g) American short grain rice
$\frac{1}{2}$ pint (250 ml) milk
$\frac{1}{4}$ pint (125 ml) orange juice
1—2 tablespoons sugar
1 oz (25 g) candied peel
6 tablespoons lemon curd, marmalade or jam

Place the rice, milk, orange juice and sugar in a heavy, non-stick saucepan and bring to the boil, stirring occasionally. Cover tightly and simmer very slowly for about 1 hour, or until the rice is tender and all the liquid has been absorbed. Stir every 10—15 minutes and check that the rice is not sticking to the pan.

Add the candied peel. Spoon the mixture into four individual ramekins, lined with clingfilm, and leave for 10 minutes. Turn out on to serving plates and serve with the warmed curd or jam poured over. Serve these chilled, if you prefer, with a hot sauce.

Sweet Treats

Kids can make lots of different sweets with rice which is already cooked. The results are better if the rice is sticky or very firm, but the sweets themselves will never become very firm and are best put straight into paper sweet cases and chilled. Here are two ideas.

Rice Nutters

Melt 4 oz (100 g) white chocolate (8 small bars) with 4 oz (100 g) left-over cooked sweet rice. Add 1 oz (25 g) dried fruit if you wish, and then leave to become firm in the fridge. Take small pieces, dip into 2 oz (50 g) finely chopped peanuts and roll into small balls. Place in paper sweet cases and chill again.

Mallow Creams

Melt 2 oz (50 g) white marshmallows and then fold in 4 oz (100 g) left-over rice pudding and a few drops of peppermint essence to taste (and a little green food colouring if you wish). Place spoonfuls of this mixture on rice paper and leave to set.

Fruit and Nut Puffovers

Serves 6

Preparation time: 25 minutes

Cooking time: 35 minutes

1 lb (450 g) puff pastry

6 oz (150 g) cold left-over rice pudding or cooked American short grain rice

1 orange, peeled and chopped

1 banana, peeled and sliced

1 oz (25 g) nuts, chopped

1 small egg, beaten

Roll out the pastry thinly to a large rectangle approximately 12 inches × 8 inches (30 cm × 20 cm) and cut into six equal-sized squares. Mix together the rice, chopped fruits and nuts and put a dessertspoonful in the middle of each square of pastry. Brush the edges of the pastry with a little beaten egg. Fold the pastry over and seal the edges, in a triangle shape. Flute the edges with your fingers and then brush with a little more beaten egg. Place the pastries on a floured baking sheet and bake in a pre-heated oven at 190°C (375°F, Gas Mark 5) for about 35 minutes. When well puffed and golden, remove from the oven and eat hot or warm.

Sweet Treats; Date Slices; Yellow Rice Cakes with
Fruity Sauce; Fruit and Nut Puffovers

Entertaining with Ease

E ntertaining has fortunately become so relaxed in recent years that you can easily ask friends in at any time of the day. Many people find that the casual American style of brunch (breakfast and early lunch combined) or a light lunch is a good way to entertain; others prefer supper parties for 10 or 12. The formal dinner party is still a good way to see only a handful of people, but you may occasionally have to put on a bigger do for 20 or more. There are ideas here for all these occasions.

Nutty Avocado Salad

Serves 4 as a starter, or 2 as a light meal with salad

Preparation time: 40 minutes (plus chilling time)

1 ripe avocado
1 tablespoon lemon juice
1 clove garlic, crushed, *or* $\frac{1}{4}$ inch (5 mm) garlic paste
1 teaspoon paprika pepper
salt and black pepper
2 tablespoons mayonnaise
4 oz (100 g) cooked chicken strips
6 oz (150 g) cooked American brown rice
1 tomato, sliced, to garnish

Cut the avocado in half, remove the stone and put all the flesh in a mixing bowl. Blend with the lemon juice, garlic, seasonings and mayonnaise. Stir in the chicken and rice and mix well. Pile the mixture back into the avocado shells if preparing only two portions, or into small ramekin dishes for four portions. Top with slices of tomato. Chill for $\frac{1}{2}$ hour before serving.

Seafood Rice en Gelée

Serves 6–8

Preparation time: 1 hour (plus chilling time)

1½ sachets (4½ teaspoons) gelatine
1 fish stock cube
1 lb (450 g) mixed fish (salmon, haddock, cod, monkfish, prawns, etc.)
a bunch of parsley
rind and juice of ½ lemon
12 oz (350 g) cooked American long grain rice
1 tablespoon tomato purée
1 tablespoon chilli sauce
¼ pint (125 ml) whipped cream
salt and black pepper
mustard and cress, a few prawns and lemon slices, to garnish

Dissolve ½ sachet (1½ teaspoons) gelatine with ⅓ fish stock cube in ¼ pint (125 ml) water. Pour into the base of a 2 pint (1 litre) ring mould or fish mould and leave to set.

Place the fish in a large pan with the remaining stock cube, a few parsley stalks, the lemon rind and juice, and 1 pint (500 ml) water. Cook gently for about 10 minutes until just cooked. Take out the fish and remove the skin and bones, returning them to the pan. Leave the fish to cool. Simmer the stock until reduced to about ⅓ pint (175 ml), then strain and sprinkle on the gelatine. When the gelatine has dissolved, set aside to cool, or place in a bowl of ice to cool more quickly.

Mix the flaked fish with the rice, tomato purée, sauce and the setting stock. Fold in 2 tablespoons chopped parsley, the whipped cream and seasoning to taste. Spoon carefully into the tin with the layer of savoury jelly in the base. Chill for several hours. Dip into boiling water for 10 seconds to release the mould, then carefully turn out and serve garnished with bunches of mustard and cress, a few whole prawns and lemon slices.

Almond-topped
Salmon Kedgeree

Serves 4

Preparation time: 40 minutes

1 tablespoon oil

1 small onion, chopped

8 oz (225 g) American long grain rice, *or* a 7 oz (200 g) packet of long grain rice with wild rice mix, cooked according to packet instructions, using the stock, wine and lemon juice

1 fish stock cube

3 tablespoons dry white wine

1 tablespoon lemon juice

1 tablespoon chopped parsley

8 oz (225 g) fresh salmon, skinned, boned and cut into small chunks

4 eggs, hard-boiled and chopped

2 oz (50 g) butter

salt and black pepper

2 oz (50 g) flaked almonds

In a large pan, heat the oil and fry the onion until translucent. Add the rice and toss over a high heat for 1 minute. Add 1 pint (500 ml) water, the stock cube, wine, lemon juice and parsley and bring to the boil. Cover tightly and simmer gently, for about 15 minutes, or until the rice is just tender.

Add the fish chunks to the rice. Cook for 5 minutes, stirring occasionally, over a very gentle heat, until the salmon is cooked. Add the eggs, butter and seasoning and mix well. Turn into a heatproof serving dish, sprinkle with the almonds and, just before serving, pop under a hot grill for 2 minutes until golden brown.

Almond-topped Salmon Kedgeree; Seafood Rice en Gelée;
Nutty Avocado Salad

Lamb Biryani

Serves 6

Preparation time: 45 minutes

Cooking time: 45 minutes

Lamb biryani is one of the oldest and most traditional dishes from the Mogul cuisine of North India. However, it is time consuming and the preparation is easiest done in stages—the spiced rice, the onions and nuts, the spiced meat and finally a spiced curd stock. These are then layered and cooked slowly together to give a delicious, delicately flavoured result.

Fortunately, it freezes well. For the best result, cook the meat in the preparation stages for at least 30 minutes. Layer as described, and then cool, seal and freeze. Cook slowly from frozen if you wish, for about 2½–3 hours.

12 oz (350 g) American long grain rice

salt

½ teaspoon saffron threads *or* 1 teaspoon turmeric

4 oz (100 g) ghee or butter

1 large onion, sliced

1 oz (25 g) slivered almonds

1 oz (25 g) shelled pistachio nuts

1 oz (25 g) California seedless raisins

1 tablespoon finely grated fresh root ginger *or* 2 tablespoons ground ginger

1 large clove garlic, crushed

1 teaspoon cumin seeds

½ teaspoon chilli powder

1½ lb (675 g) lean lamb, diced

4 inch (10 cm) piece cinnamon stick

8 cloves

2 teaspoons crushed black peppercorns

½ teaspoon ground coriander

½ teaspoon ground mace

½ teaspoon ground nutmeg

¼ pint (125 ml) beef or lamb stock	
6 tablespoons natural yogurt	
6 tablespoons double cream	
extra nuts, to garnish	

Place the rice, ½ teaspoon of salt and the saffron or turmeric in a pan with 1½ pints (750 ml) boiling water. Cover tightly and simmer for 15 minutes, when all the liquid should have been absorbed.

Melt the ghee or butter in a large, heavy-based pan and gently fry the onion slices until translucent. Remove them carefully with a draining spoon and set aside on kitchen paper. Fry the nuts and raisins gently in the butter until the nuts are just golden. Transfer them to the kichen paper too.

To the fat, add the ginger, garlic, cumin seeds and chilli powder and fry for 1 minute. Then add the lamb and toss over a high heat for 5 minutes until browned. Add the cinnamon, cloves, black peppercorns, coriander, mace, nutmeg and stock, cover tightly and simmer for 15 minutes. Drain the meat juices into another dish and add the yogurt and the cream.

To assemble, layer the onions, rice, nuts and lamb in a good-sized casserole dish with a lid. Finally, pour over the creamy stock and cover tightly. Cook in a pre-heated oven at 190°C (375°F, Gas Mark 5) for about 20 minutes. Serve, either as it is, straight from the casserole, or pile the biryani on to a large, flat, heated serving plate and sprinkle with a few extra pistachios and almonds.

Trout Fillets in Mustard Rice

Serves 4 as a starter, or 2 as a light meal

Preparation time: 1 hour 20 minutes

Cooking time: 30 minutes

For a starter, these are nicest done in small ramekin dishes and carefully turned out. For a light meal you may prefer to cook them all in one dish and serve two fillets per person, in which case the fillets need to be tightly packed into a shallow dish and covered with the rice.

2 trout (about 9 oz (250 g) each), skinned and filleted

3 oz (75 g) American long grain rice, cooked, and 1 oz (25 g) American wild rice, cooked, *or* 4 oz (100 g) long grain and wild rice mix, cooked

2 tablespoons parsley

2 tablespoons Meaux mustard or other grainy mustard

2 tablespoons lemon juice

salt and black pepper

1 oz (25 g) butter, softened

4 tablespoons dry Vermouth

sprigs of parsley, to garnish

Roll up the skinned trout fillets neatly. Mix the rice with the parsley, 1 tablespoon mustard, lemon juice and seasoning. Thickly grease the inside and base of four small ramekin dishes with the butter and then spread a layer of the remaining mustard on to the butter. Line the dishes with some of the rice, pressing it well into the mustard and butter coating. Place a fillet in each dish and pack in the rest of the rice so that the fillets are well surrounded and topped with rice. Pour a little Vermouth over each one. Cover with foil and bake in a pre-heated oven at 200°C (400°F, Gas Mark 6) for 30 minutes.

Leave to settle for 5 minutes before turning out on to serving dishes. Garnish with sprigs of parsley.

Lamb Biryani; Trout Fillets in Mustard Rice

Paella

Although paella is probably Spain's most famous dish, it would be impossible ever to get the same result each time you eat or cook it. Every household and every region would add a different speciality, and so, like a good curry, it depends almost entirely on the cook and the food available in the market that day. A paella is particularly good cooked in the open over a barbecue, so that it can have a very fast cooking at the beginning, and a long, slow cooking afterwards. However you cook it, you should never stir it during the slow cooking stage as that only lets out the heat! It is an ideal dish for entertaining crowds, and can make a stunning centrepiece for a buffet table.

2 large chickens or rabbits
salt and pepper
1 lb (450 g) garbanzos or chick peas, soaked overnight
2 lb (1 kg) mussels, scrubbed and cleaned
olive oil
4 red or green peppers, de-seeded and sliced
8—9 cloves garlic, chopped
2 lb (1 kg) tomatoes, quartered
4 tablespoons parsley
4 lb (2 kg) American long grain rice
a few strands of saffron *or* ½ teaspoon turmeric powder
20 large prawns
lemon wedges and chopped parsley, to garnish

Clean the chickens or rabbits and cut into about 20 small portions. Boil in seasoned water for 20—30 minutes, or until just tender. Leave in the pan until required.

Drain the garbanzos, place in a large pan with fresh water, bring to the boil and simmer for 1—1½ hours or until tender. Leave in the pan until required.

Cook the mussels in a large pan with only about ½ pint (250 ml) water, for 7—8 minutes. Toss the pan occasionally, with the lid on to shake them around. They are ready when the shells open. (Discard any that do not open.) Leave in the pan until required.

In a large pan, heat 4 tablespoons oil and fry the peppers until golden. Add the garlic, tomatoes, parsley, rice, seasoning, chicken portions, garbanzos and about 1 pint (500 ml) of either cooking liquid. If using saffron, soften the strands in 3 tablespoons of boiling stock, leave for 2—3 minutes and strain into the pan. Add the turmeric powder if you are using that instead.

Bring to the boil, stirring occasionally. Then either cover the pan and cook slowly on the top of the cooker, or transfer the paella to a paella dish or very large, shallow ovenproof dish, cover with foil and bake in a pre-heated oven at 180°C (350°F, Gas Mark 4) for about 1 hour. Check occasionally that it is not drying out and add more of either cooking liquid as necessary. When the rice is nearly tender, add the mussels and prawns, burying them in so that they heat through. Finally, serve with wedges of lemon and sprinkled with lots of parsley.

Rice-coated Prawn Balls

Makes 20—24

Preparation time: 50 minutes (plus chilling time)

Cooking time: 20 minutes

Ⓕ

1 small slice white bread

5 teaspoons fish stock or water

12 oz (350 g) shelled prawns

1 oz (25 g) pork fat or butter or lemon-flavoured butter

½ teaspoon grated fresh root ginger

1 tablespoon lemon juice

1 oz (25 g) nibbed almonds

salt and black pepper

1 small egg yolk

1 oz (25 g) cornflour

2 small egg whites, lightly beaten

12—14 oz (350—400 g) cooked American long grain rice, chopped*

oil, for frying

1 small green pepper, thinly sliced, and wedges of lemon, to garnish

*Dry, loose grains of rice can be chopped easily and quickly in a food processor, for only about 1 minute.

Soak the bread in the stock or water until all the liquid is absorbed. Put aside 2 oz (50 g) prawns for garnish. Mash the rest of the prawns with the bread, fat, ginger, lemon juice, almonds, seasoning and egg yolk. When well blended, shape and roll the mixture into about 20 or more balls (depending on the size you choose).

Toss the balls lightly in cornflour, then in egg white and then in the rice. Roll them in your hands once more to give them a good shape and then chill them for 2 hours.

Deep fry 5 or 6 at a time in hot oil, for about 5 minutes or until golden all over and slightly crisp. Drain on kitchen paper and then serve with slices of green pepper, deep fried, a few of the remaining prawns and a wedge of lemon. For a buffet or cocktail nibbles, just serve with slices or wedges of lemon.

Paella; Rice-coated Prawn Balls

Duck with Pomegranate and Wild Rice

Serves 4
Preparation time: 55 minutes
Cooking time: 1 hour 35 minutes

Pomegranates are usually only available in the autumn and winter. Although they are fiddly to eat raw, they are not too fiddly to use for cooking or for their juice, as in this recipe. Their rich, slightly sharp flavour goes very well with the duck and also adds a slightly perfumed, exotic touch, typical of the Middle East where pomegranates are used often.

1 × 4–4½ lb (2–2.25 kg) duck
salt and pepper
2 oz (50 g) American wild rice
4 oz (100 g) American brown rice
4 oz (100 g) American long grain rice
a little olive oil
3 shallots, chopped
1 large clove garlic, crushed
1 tablespoon lemon juice
1 teaspoon chopped parsley
2 pomegranates
3–4 tablespoons red wine
1 teaspoon cornflour
¼ pint (125 ml) chicken stock
watercress, to garnish

Wash the duck and wipe dry. Remove the giblets if they are included and simmer with ½ pint (250 ml) water for about 20 minutes to give a stock for use in the gravy or soups. Prick the skin of the duck thoroughly all over and place the duck on a trivet in a roasting tin. Sprinkle with seasoning and roast in a pre-heated oven at 190°C (375°F, Gas Mark 5) for about 1½ hours, or until the juices run clear when you prick the flesh. Baste the duck with its own fat several times during cooking to encourage browning.

Place the wild and brown rice in a large pan with ¾ pint (375 ml) salted boiling water and simmer, tightly covered, for 25 minutes, stirring occasionally. Add the long grain rice and a further ½ pint (250 ml) boiling water to the pan and continue cooking, covered, for another 15—20 minutes. All the rices should by now be cooked and the water absorbed. If not quite dry, remove the pan lid and continue cooking for just a few minutes more.

Meanwhile, heat the oil and gently fry the shallots and garlic until translucent. Add the lemon juice and parsley. Cut one of the pomegranates in half, then break it into smaller pieces and gently ease out the bright red seeds separately. Remove any of the yellow strands of shell. Add these seeds to the shallots along with the cooked rice, and toss them all well together. Keep the rice mixture warm while preparing the sauce.

Using a juice extractor, squeeze out the juice of the second pomegranate. Place the cooked duck on its serving dish. Drain most of the fat from the roasting tin, leaving only 1—2 tablespoons of the sediment. To this, add the pomegranate juice, the red wine and the cornflour dissolved in ¼ pint (125 ml) giblet or chicken stock. Bring slowly to the boil, stirring well and then cook for 2 minutes until slightly thickened and smooth. Surround the duck with the finished rice, garnish with watercress and serve the pomegranate sauce separately.

Cheese and Chive Soufflés

Serves 6

Preparation time: 25 minutes

Cooking time: 30 minutes

Ⓕ (uncooked)

4 oz (100 g) American long grain rice, cooked as directed on page 7

1 oz (25 g) butter

4 oz (100 g) fresh cream cheese or fresh soft cheese (*fromage frais*) or fresh goat's cheese (*chèvre*)

1 teaspoon chive mustard

2 eggs, separated

¼ pint (125 ml) double cream

salt and pepper

2 teaspoons fresh chives, chopped

Toss the hot rice immediately in butter. In a food processor, blend together the rice, cheese, mustard, egg yolks and cream. (If you don't have a processor, cream the cheese and cream together and then beat in the other ingredients.) Whisk the egg whites until stiff. Season the rice mixture to taste, stir in half the chopped chives and then fold in the whisked egg whites.

Spoon the mixture into six greased, individual ramekin dishes and flatten the tops. Sprinkle with the remaining chives and bake in a pre-heated oven at 180°C (350°F, Gas Mark 4) for 25—30 minutes or until well risen and golden. Serve immediately.

Duck with Pomegranate and Wild Rice;
Cheese and Chive Soufflés

Spicy Stuffed Mussels

Serves 4 as a starter

Preparation time: 40 minutes

Cooking time: 35 minutes

This combination of rice, shellfish, spices and dried fruit is Turkish.
Although is is an unusual mixture, no one flavour overpowers the
others and it produces a deliciously moist and tasty hot or cold
starter.

2—3 tablespoons olive oil

1 medium onion, chopped

4 oz (100 g) American long grain rice

1 oz (25 g) pine kernels

1 tablespoon California seedless raisins

$\frac{1}{4}$ teaspoon ground cinnamon

a pinch of ground allspice

salt and pepper

1—1$\frac{1}{4}$ lb (450—600 g) mussels in their shells (you need about 8 for
each person)

$\frac{1}{2}$ vegetable stock cube

$\frac{1}{4}$ pint (125 ml) dry white wine

In a saucepan with a lid, heat the oil and gently cook the onion until
translucent. Add the rice, pine kernels, raisins, spices and seasoning
and $\frac{1}{2}$ pint (250 ml) boiling water. Cook gently, covered, for 15
minutes, stirring occasionally to make sure the rice does not dry out
completely.

Scrub clean the mussels and discard any that are open or cracked
and split. With a very thin, small, sharp knife, carefully prize open
the shells from the thick end but leaving the thinner end still hinged.
Loosen the mussel flesh with a blunt knife.

Place 1 teaspoon of the cooked rice mixture into each mussel,
ease them nearly closed again and pack tightly in a shallow,
ovenproof dish. Mix the stock cube with $\frac{1}{4}$ pint (125 ml) boiling
water and the wine and pour over the mussels. Cover tightly with
foil and bake in a pre-heated oven at 190°C (375°F, Gas Mark 5) for
20 minutes.

Serve hot with french bread, or allow to cool and then chill before
serving.

Dolmades

Makes 40

Preparation time: 1 hour

Cooking time: 45 minutes

5—6 tablespoons olive oil

1 onion, finely chopped

1 clove garlic, crushed

3 oz (75 g) American long grain rice

salt and black pepper

40 vine leaves or small cabbage leaves

1 oz (25 g) sunflower seeds, toasted

1 tangerine, peeled, segmented and chopped

1 oz (25 g) bunch of fresh coriander or parsley, chopped

3—4 tablespoons lemon juice

¼ pint (125 ml) tomato juice

lemon wedges, to garnish

In a large pan, heat 2 tablespoons of the oil and fry the onion and garlic until translucent. Add the rice and toss until translucent. Sprinkle with a little salt, add 6 fl oz (175 ml) water and bring to the boil. Cover tightly and simmer, very gently, for 15 minutes, or until the rice is tender and quite dry.

Meanwhile, blanch the vine or cabbage leaves in boiling, salted water, for only 1 minute each. Drain on kitchen paper, and lay them dull side upwards.

To the rice, add the sunflower seeds, chopped tangerine, chopped coriander or parsley, seasoning, 1 tablespoon of oil and 1 tablespoon of lemon juice. Mix well and place a small spoonful of the mixture in the middle of each vine or cabbage leaf. Fold and roll up the leaves neatly into small cylinders and arrange, edges downwards, in an oiled casserole dish, in layers. Sprinkle with seasoning, the rest of the oil, 2—3 tablespoons of lemon juice and the tomato juice. Cover tightly, bring to the boil, and simmer gently for 45 minutes. Alternatively, cook in a pre-heated oven at 180°C (350°F, Gas Mark 4).

Serve hot, or chill well and serve on one large platter with wedges of lemon.

Escalopes with Nutty Centres

Serves 4

Preparation time: 1 hour 10 minutes

Cooking time: 35 minutes

1 oz (25 g) American wild rice, cooked as directed on page 7

4 oz (100 g) American long grain rice, cooked as directed on page 7

1 tablespoon oil

1 oz (25 g) butter

1 small onion, chopped

1 clove garlic, crushed

2 oz (50 g) salted cashew nuts

salt and black pepper

4 slices veal escalope, pork leg or turkey breast, beaten out until very thin

$\frac{1}{4}$ pint (125 ml) home-made, canned or bottled tomato sauce

6 tablespoons double cream

6 tablespoons water

4 tablespoons dry Martini

4 wedges of lemon, to serve

Mix the rices together. Heat the oil and butter together and cook the onion and garlic until translucent. Add the rice, most of the nuts (saving a few for garnishing) and seasoning. Lay out the escalopes flat and divide the filling evenly between them. Roll up carefully from one end and tie in two places with string. Place in a shallow, ovenproof dish.

Mix together the tomato sauce, cream, water and dry Martini and pour over the escalopes. Cover with foil and cook in a pre-heated oven at 180°C (350°F, Gas Mark 4) for 35–40 minutes. Remove the string before serving, sprinkle with the remaining nuts and serve with the lemon wedges.

Escalopes with Nutty Centres;
Spicy Stuffed Mussels; Dolmades

Corn Mountain with Prawns and Pimento Sauce

Serves 4 as a light meal

Preparation time: 50 minutes

This is perfect for a buffet table and, if you can carefully arrange the prawns up the mountain, it looks most attractive. However, try to serve it out yourself or you will find people take too many prawns!

8 oz (225 g) American long grain rice, cooked as directed on page 7

8 oz (225 g) sweetcorn kernels

1 yellow or orange pepper, de-seeded, chopped and blanched

2 tablespoons chopped chives

4 oz (100 g) garlic butter or herb and black pepper flavoured butter, melted

salt

1 lb (450 g) prawns (with shells) and wedges of lemon, to serve

PIMENTO SAUCE:

$\frac{1}{4}$ pint (125 ml) bottled pimento sauce; *or* $2\frac{1}{2}$ fl oz (75 ml) real mayonnaise, $2\frac{1}{2}$ fl oz (75 ml) whipped cream, 1 tablespoon paprika pepper, seasoning and a few drops of Tabasco sauce, blended together

To the hot rice, add the corn, pepper, chives, butter and seasoning to taste. Pack tightly into a $1\frac{1}{2}$–2 lb (0.75–1 kg) clingfilm-lined pudding basin or high mould. Leave for about 15 minutes, and then turn out on to a serving plate. Surround or decorate with the whole prawns and wedges of lemon. Serve with the sauce (and finger bowls!).

Noisettes in Rice Nests with Mint Bearnaise Sauce

Serves 4
Preparation time: 50 minutes
Cooking time: about 10 minutes

6 oz (150 g) cooked American long grain rice
1 oz (25 g) butter, melted
salt and pepper
2 tablespoons mint jelly
1 tablespoon chopped fresh mint *or* 1 teaspoon dried mint
4 lamb cutlets (best end chops), boned, rolled and tied into noisettes
a little oil

MINT BEARNAISE SAUCE:
3 tablespoons mint sauce
1 teaspoon Dijon mustard
1 teaspoon lemon juice
2 egg yolks
4 oz (100 g) butter, cut into pieces
1 teaspoon chopped parsley, to serve

Thoroughly mix together the rice, melted butter, seasoning, jelly and chopped mint. Divide the mixture into four and pack it into four individual sponge flan tins, quiche tins, rum baba tins or shell-shaped dishes. Place in a warm oven until required.

Lightly oil and season the lamb noisettes and grill them for 4–7 minutes each side (depending on how pink you like the lamb).

To prepare the sauce, simmer the mint sauce, mustard and lemon juice together until reduced to 2 teaspoons. Transfer it to a double saucepan, or a bowl over hot water, and whisk in the egg yolks. Cook, stirring all the time, until the sauce coats the back of a wooden spoon. Then gradually whisk in the butter until you have a thickened, glossy sauce.

To serve, turn the rice nests out on to heated serving plates, place a noisette in the centre of each one, pour a little sauce over and sprinkle with parsley. Serve the rest of the sauce separately.

Lemon Rice Caramel

Serves 8

Preparation time: 35 minutes

Cooking time: 1 hour

As with crème caramels, this dessert can be prepared in individual dishes well in advance, ready just to turn out at the last moment and serve chilled.

6 oz (150 g) granulated sugar

6 tablespoons water

4 oz (100 g) American short grain rice

1½ pints (750 ml) milk

¼ pint (125 ml) double cream

3 eggs

3 teaspoons grated lemon rind

1—2 tablespoons lemon juice

sugar, to taste

In a small, heavy-based pan, place the sugar and the water and heat very gently to dissolve the sugar. When thoroughly dissolved, bring to the boil, and boil the syrup gently, without stirring, until it begins to turn golden. Remove from the heat immediately, allow to darken a little more, and pour into the base of a 2 pint (1 litre) ring mould or flan dish. Swirl the tin around so that the caramel coats the sides.

Cook the rice in the milk as directed on page 7, for about 25 minutes. Cool slightly before stirring in the cream, eggs, lemon rind and juice, and sugar to taste. Spoon this into the caramel-lined tin. Bake slowly in a pre-heated oven at 170°C (325°F, Gas Mark 3) for about 1 hour, or until just firm to the touch.

Turn out into a shallow serving dish and serve hot or cold.

Noisettes in Rice Nests with Mint Bearnaise Sauce;
Lemon Rice Caramel

Raspberry Rice Ring

Serves 6—8

Preparation time: 1 hour (plus chilling time)

4 oz (100 g) American short grain rice

1 pint (500 ml) milk

1 sachet (3 teaspoons) gelatine

1 lb (450 g) fresh or frozen raspberries

4 tablespoons raspberry, strawberry or blackcurrant liqueur

4—6 tablespoons sugar, or to taste

2 tablespoons lemon juice

¼ pint (125 ml) double cream, whipped

Cook the rice in the milk as directed on page 7 for about 45 minutes, until softened. Immediately sprinkle on the gelatine and stir it in. Leave for 5—10 minutes to dissolve in the heat of the rice. Blend, liquidise or process the rice with 6 oz (150 g) raspberries, liqueur, sugar to taste and lemon juice for only a few minutes to give a slightly smoother consistency. Cool slightly, fold in the whipped cream and spoon into a clingfilm-lined 2 pint (1 litre) savarin or ring mould or tin. Chill for several hours.

Turn out and fill the hollow with the remaining raspberries.

Jewels in a Crown

Serves 6—8

Preparation time: 35 minutes (plus chilling time)

4 oz (100 g) American short grain rice

1 pint (500 ml) milk

7 oz (200 g) cream cheese

10 oz (275 g) mixed glacé and dried fruits, chopped

2 oz (50 g) nuts, chopped

3—4 tablespooons sugar, or to taste

a few drops vanilla essence

¼ pint (125 ml) double cream, softly whipped

1 tablespoon liqueur (try Amaretto, Tia Maria or Drambuie), to serve

Cook the rice in the milk as directed on page 7 for about 35 minutes, until softened. Allow to cool slightly and then mix in the cheese, fruit, nuts, sugar to taste and vanilla essence. Finally, fold in the softly whipped cream. Spoon into a clingfilm-lined 2 pint (1 litre) mould or pudding basin. Chill for several hours.

Turn out and serve with the liqueur poured over.

Iced Rice Cheesecake

Serves 6—8

Preparation time: 30 minutes (plus chilling time)

1 sachet (3 teaspoons) gelatine

14 oz (400 g) can apricot halves in juice

4 oz (100 g) American short grain rice, cooked as directed on page 7 in ¾ pint (375 ml) milk

8 oz (225 g) cottage cheese

juice and grated rind of ½ lemon

3—4 tablespoons honey, or to taste

¼ pint (125 ml) double cream, whipped

2 egg whites, stiffly whisked

cocoa powder, to decorate

Dissolve the gelatine in 3 tablespoons of the apricot juice and set aside. Drain off the rest of the apricot juice (for other uses), put aside six apricot halves for decoration and put the rest in a bowl or the base of a food processor. Add the cooked rice, cheese, lemon juice and rind, and honey. Blend or liquidise for 2—3 minutes until slightly smoother (or continue until very smooth if you prefer).

Transfer to a large mixing bowl and add the gelatine. Fold in the cream and whisked egg whites. Spoon into a clingfilm-lined 2 pint (1 litre) mould or tin and chill for several hours.

Turn out on to a serving plate and sprinkle with very finely sifted cocoa powder. Decorate with the remaining apricot halves. Serve lightly iced (½ hour in the freezer).

Brandy Rice Alaska

Serves 8

Preparation time: 50 minutes

Cooking time: 1 hour 10 minutes

4 oz (100 g) American short grain rice

1 pint (500 ml) milk

a few drops vanilla essence

4 tablespoons brandy

¼ pint (125 ml) double cream

3 eggs, separated

sugar, to taste

1 ripe mango, peeled and chopped

4 oz (100 g) white grapes, peeled and pipped

6 oz (150 g) caster sugar

Cook the rice in the milk as directed on page 7, but for only about 25 minutes. Stir in the vanilla essence, brandy, cream, egg yolks and sugar to taste. Add the chopped flesh of the mango and half the grapes to the rice. Spoon into a 2 pint (1 litre) pudding dish or mould and bake in a pre-heated oven at 170°C (325°F, Gas Mark 3) for 1 hour. Remove from the oven and allow to stand for 15 minutes.

Whisk the egg whites until stiff, whisk in half the sugar gently and then fold in the rest. Turn the pudding out on to a heatproof serving dish and spread the meringue, in swirls, over the top. Put in a pre-heated oven at 220°C (425°F, Gas Mark 7) for 5—8 minutes or until golden all over. Serve decorated with the remaining grapes.